Oracle Regular Expressions
Pocket Reference

Jonathan Gennick and Peter Linsley

Beijing · Cambridge · Farnham · Köln · Sebastopol · Tokyo

Oracle Regular Expressions Pocket Reference
by Jonathan Gennick and Peter Linsley

Published by O'Reilly & Associates, Inc., 1005 Gravenstein Highway North, Sebastopol, CA 95472.

O'Reilly & Associates books may be purchased for educational, business, or sales promotional use. Online editions are also available for most titles (*safari.oreilly.com*). For more information, contact our corporate/institutional sales department: (800) 998-9938 or *corporate@oreilly.com*.

Editor:	Deborah Russell
Production Editor:	Philip Dangler
Cover Designer:	Emma Colby
Interior Designer:	David Futato

Printing History:

September 2003:   First Edition.

978-0-596-00601-3
[LSI]   [2011-06-24]

Contents

Oracle Regular Expressions Pocket Reference

Introduction

With the release of Oracle Database 10g, Oracle has introduced regular expression support to the company's flagship product. Regular expressions are used to describe patterns in text, and they are an invaluable aid when working with loosely formatted textual data.

This little booklet describes Oracle's regular expression support in detail. Its goal is to enable you to take full advantage of the newly introduced regular expression features when querying and manipulating textual data.

Organization of This Book

This book is divided into the following six sections:

Introduction
> You're reading it now.

Tutorial
> Provides a short regular expression tutorial aimed at those who aren't already familiar with regular expressions.

Oracle's Regular Expression Support
> For readers familiar with regular expressions, describes how they are implemented and used within Oracle. Also includes a description of the key differences between the regular expression implementations of Perl and Oracle.

Regular Expression Quick Reference
Describes the regular expression metacharacters supported by Oracle and provides examples of their usage.

Oracle Regular Expression Functions
Details the new SQL and PL/SQL functions that make up Oracle's regular expression support.

Oracle Regular Expression Error Messages
Lists all of Oracle's regular expression error messages and provides advice as to what do when you encounter a given message.

Conventions

The following typographical conventions are used in this book:

UPPERCASE
Indicates a SQL or PL/SQL keyword

lowercase
Indicates a user-defined item, such as a table name or a column name, in a SQL or PL/SQL statement

Italic
Indicates URLs, emphasis, or the introduction of new technical terms

Constant width
Used for code examples and for in-text references to table names, column names, regular expressions, and so forth

Constant width bold
Indicates user input in code examples showing both input and output

Acknowledgments

We thank Debby Russell and Todd Mezzulo of O'Reilly & Associates for believing in and supporting this book. We also thank Barry Trute, Michael Yau, Weiran Zhang, Keni Matsuda, Ken Jacobs, and the others at Oracle Corporation who spent valuable time reviewing this manuscript to ensure its accuracy.

Peter would like to acknowledge Weiran Zhang for his finesse and intellect as codeveloper of Oracle's regular expression features. Peter would also like to thank Ritsu for being an ever-supportive and encouraging wife.

Jonathan would like to thank Dale Bowen for providing the Spanish sentence used for the collation example; Andrew Sears for spending so much time with Jeff; Jeff for dragging his dad on so many bike rides to the Falling Rock Cafe for ice cream and coffee; and the Falling Rock Cafe for, well, just for being there.

Example Data

Many of the example SQL statements in this book execute against the following table:

```
CREATE TABLE park (
    park_name NVARCHAR2 (40),
    park_phone NVARCHAR2 (15),
    country VARCHAR2 (2),
    description NCLOB
);
```

This table contains information on a variety of state, provincial, and national parks from around the world. Much of the information is in free-text form within the description column, making this table an ideal platform on which to demonstrate Oracle's regular expression capabilities.

You can download a script to create the park table and populate it with data from *http://oreilly.com/catalog/oracleregex*.

Tutorial

A *regular expression* (often known as a *regex*) is a sequence of characters that describe a pattern in text. Regular expressions use a syntax that has evolved over a number of years, and that is now codified as part of the POSIX standard.

Regular expressions are extremely useful, because they allow you to work with text in terms of patterns. For example, you can use regular expressions to search the park table and identify any park with a description containing text that looks like a phone number. You can then use the same regular expression to extract that phone number from the description.

NOTE

This tutorial will get you started using regular expressions, but we can only begin to cover the topic in this small book. If you want to learn about regular expressions in depth, see Jeffrey Friedl's excellent book *Mastering Regular Expressions* (O'Reilly).

Patterns

The simplest type of *pattern* is simply an exact string of characters that you are searching for, such as the string in the following WHERE clause:

```
SELECT *
FROM park
WHERE park_name='Mackinac Island State Park';
```

However, the string 'Mackinac Island State Park' isn't what most people think of when you mention the word "pattern." The expectation is that a pattern will use so-called *metacharacters* that allow for matches when you know only the general pattern of text you are looking for.

Standard SQL has long had rather limited support for pattern matching in the form of the LIKE predicate. For example, the

---

following query attempts to return the names of all state parks:

```
SELECT park_name
FROM park
WHERE park_name LIKE '%State Park%';
```

The percent (%) characters in this pattern specify that any number of characters are allowed on either side of the string 'State Park'. Any number of characters may be zero characters, so strings in the form 'xxx State Park' fit the pattern. There! I've just used a pattern to describe the operation of a pattern.

NOTE

Humans have long used patterns as a way to organize and describe text. Look no further than your address and phone number for examples of commonly used patterns.

Handy as it is at times, LIKE is an amazingly weak predicate, supporting only two expression metacharacters that don't even begin to address the range of patterns you might need to describe in your day-to-day work. You need more. You need a richer and more expressive language for describing patterns. You need regular expressions.

Regular Expressions

Regular expressions is the answer to the question: "How do I describe a pattern of text?" Regular expressions first became widely used on the Unix platform, supported by such utilities as *ed*, *grep*, and (notably) Perl. Regular expressions have gone on to become formalized in the IEEE POSIX standard, and regular expressions are widely supported across an ever-growing range of editors, email clients, programming languages, scripting languages, and now Oracle SQL and PL/SQL.

Let's revisit the earlier problem of finding state parks in the park table. We performed that task using LIKE to search for the words 'State Park' in the park_name column. Following is the regular expression solution to the problem:

```
SELECT park_name
FROM park
WHERE REGEXP_LIKE(park_name, 'State Park');
```

REGEXP_LIKE is a new Oracle predicate that searches, in this case, the park_name column to see whether it contains a string matching the pattern 'State Park'. REGEXP_LIKE is similar to LIKE, but differs in one major respect: LIKE requires its pattern to match the entire column value, whereas REGEXP_LIKE looks for its pattern anywhere within the column value.

There are no metacharacters in the regular expression 'State Park', so it's not a terribly exciting pattern. Following is a more interesting example that attempts to identify parks with descriptions containing phone numbers:

```
SELECT park_name
FROM park
WHERE REGEXP_LIKE(description, '...-....');
```

This query uses the regular expression metacharacter period (.), which matches any character. The expression does not look for three periods followed by a dash followed by four periods. It looks for any three characters, followed by a dash, followed by any four characters. Because it matches any character, the period is a very commonly used regular expression metacharacter.

NOTE

You can create function-based indexes to support queries using REGEXP_LIKE and other REGEXP functions in the WHERE clause.

It can be inconvenient to specify repetition by repeating the metacharacter, so regular expression syntax allows you to follow a metacharacter with an indication of how many times you want that metacharacter to be repeated. For example:

```
SELECT park_name
FROM park
WHERE REGEXP_LIKE(description, '.{3}-.{4}');
```

The *interval quantifier* {3} is used to specify that the first period should repeat three times. The {4} following the second period indicates a repeat count of four. This pattern of a regular expression syntax element followed by a quantifier is one you'll frequently encounter and use when working with regular expressions.

Table 1 illustrates the types of quantifiers you can use to specify repetition in a regular expression. The later "Regular Expression Quick Reference" section describes each of these quantifiers in detail.

Table 1. Quantifiers used to specify repetition in a pattern

Pattern	Matches
.*	Zero or more characters
.+	One or more characters
.?	Zero or one character
.{3,4}	Three to four characters
.{3,}	Three or more characters
.{3}	Exactly three characters

Bracket Expressions

The examples in the previous section searched for phone numbers using the period (.). That's not a very precise search, because the period matches any character, not just digits. A phrase such as 'A 217-acre park...' will result in a false positive, because '217-acre' fits the '...-....' pattern. The following query uses REGEXP_SUBSTR to extract the text matching the pattern so that you can see the false positives that result:

```
SELECT park_name,
       REGEXP_SUBSTR(description, '...-....')
FROM park;
```

If you've downloaded the example data for this book and are following along, execute the above query and look at the results for Färnebofjärden and Muskallonge Lake State Park, among others.

NOTE

If you're ever in doubt as to why REGEXP_LIKE reports the existence of a given pattern in a text value, use REGEXP_SUBSTR to extract that same pattern from the value in question, and you'll see the text REGEXP_LIKE considered a match for your pattern.

Regular expression syntax provides several ways for you to be more specific about the characters you are searching for. One approach is to specify a list of characters in square brackets ([ ]):

```
SELECT park_name
FROM park
WHERE REGEXP_LIKE(description,
    '[0123456789]{3}-[0123456789]{4}');
```

Square brackets and their contents are referred to as *bracket expressions*, and define a specific subset of characters, any one of which can provide a single-character match. In this example, the bracket expressions each define the set of characters comprising the digits 0–9. Following each list is a repeat count, either {3} or {4}.

It's painful to have to type out each of the digits 0–9, and it's error-prone too, as you might skip a digit. A better solution is to specify a range of characters:

```
SELECT park_name
FROM park
WHERE REGEXP_LIKE(description, '[0-9]{3}-[0-9]{4}');
```

Even better, perhaps, in this case, is to use one of the named character classes:

```
SELECT park_name
FROM park
WHERE REGEXP_LIKE(description,
    '[[:digit:]]{3}-[[:digit:]]{4}');
```

Named character classes such as [:digit:] are especially important in multilingual environments, because they enable you to write expressions that work across languages and character sets.

NOTE

Character classes are supported only within bracket expressions. Thus you cannot write [:digit:]{3}, but instead must use [[:digit:]]{3}.

You can even define a set of characters in terms of what it is not. The following example uses [^[:digit:]] to allow for any character other than a digit to separate the groups of a phone number:

```
SELECT park_name
FROM park
WHERE REGEXP_LIKE(description,
    '[[:digit:]]{3}[^[:digit:]][[:digit:]]{4}');
```

Any time you specify a caret (^) as the first character within a bracket expression, you are telling the regular expression engine to begin by including all possible characters in the set, and to then exclude only those that you list following the caret.

NOTE

Most metacharacters lose their special meaning when used within a bracket expression. See "[ ] (Square Brackets)" in the "Regular Expression Quick Reference" section for details on this issue.

Bracket expressions can be much more complex and varied than those we've shown so far. For example, the following bracket expression:

```
[[:digit:]A-Zxyza-c]
```

includes all digits, the uppercase letters A through Z, lowercase x, y, and z, and lowercase a through c.

The Escape Character

So far you've seen that periods (.), square brackets ([ ]), and braces ({}) all have special meaning in a regular expression. But these are common characters! What if you are searching specifically for one of these characters rather than what it represents?

If you look carefully at the various park descriptions, you'll see that some phone numbers are delimited using periods rather than hyphens. For example, the Tahquamenon Falls State Park phone number is given as 906.492.3415. With one exception, the pattern we've been using so far demands a hyphen between digit groups:

```
[[:digit:]]{3}-[[:digit:]]{4}
```

To find phone numbers delimited by periods, you might think you could simply place a period between digit groups:

```
[[:digit:]]{3}.[[:digit:]]{4}
```

However, the period in this case would be interpreted as a wildcard, and would match any character—a dash, a period, or something else. To specify that you really do mean a period, and not the wildcard match that a period represents, you need to *escape* the period by preceding it with a backslash (\):

```
SELECT park_name
FROM park
WHERE REGEXP_LIKE(description,
                  '[[:digit:]]{3}\.[[:digit:]]{4}');
```

This query will now find only parks with phone numbers delimited by periods in the description column. The \. tells the regular expression engine to look for a literal period.

Any time you want to use one of the regular expression meta-characters as a regular character, you must precede it with a backslash. If you want to use a backslash as a regular character, precede it with another backslash, as in \\.

Be aware that the list of metacharacters changes inside square brackets ([ ]). Most lose their special meaning, and do not need to be escaped. See the quick reference subsection on square brackets for details on this issue.

Subexpressions

Earlier you saw quantifiers used to specify the number of repetitions for a metacharacter. For example, we first used .{3} to specify that phone numbers begin with three characters. Later we used [[:digit:]]{3} to specify that phone numbers begin with three digits. However, what if you want to specify a repeat count for not just a single metacharacter or bracket expression, but for any arbitrary part of a subexpression?

You can apply a quantifier to any arbitrary part of an expression simply by enclosing that part of the expression in parentheses. The result is called a *subexpression*, and you can follow a subexpression with a quantifier to specify repetition.

For example, the regular expression in the following query searches for non-U.S. phone numbers. It does this by looking for a plus sign (+) followed by two to five groups of 1–3 digits, with each group of 1–3 digits being followed by a single space:

```
SELECT park_name,
       REGEXP_SUBSTR(description,
          '\+([0-9]{1,3} ){1,4}([0-9]+)') intl_phone
FROM park;
```

```
Färnebofjärden                +46 8 698 10 00
Mackinac Island State Park    ***Null***
Fort Wilkins State Park       ***Null***
...
```

The first interval expression, {1,3}, refers to [0-9], and matches 1–3 digits. The second interval expression, {2,4}, refers to the subexpression maching 1–3 digits plus one space. Finally, we use the subexpression ([0-9]*) to pick up a final digit group without also including a trailing space in our results.

In this example, we require at least two digit groups, one from the first subexpression and one from the second, in an attempt to reduce false positives. In our experience, non-U.S. phone numbers are most frequently written with at least two digit groups.

NOTE

In the end, you can't always be sure that text matching a pattern has the semantics, or meaning, that you want. See the later section, "Fuzziness."

Alternation

Humans don't like to follow rules, and just when you think you've got a pattern nailed down, you'll discover that someone is using a variation on the pattern, or perhaps a completely different pattern. For example, in the previous section we began to deal with the fact that some of the phone numbers in the park descriptions use periods rather than dashes to separate the digit groups.

Regular expression syntax supports a concept called *alternation*, which simply means that you can specify alternative versions of a pattern. Alternation in a regular expression is like the OR operator in the SELECT statement's WHERE clause.

You specify alternation using a vertical bar (|) to separate two alternatives, either of which is acceptable. For example:

```
SELECT park_name
FROM park
WHERE REGEXP_LIKE(description,
    '[[:digit:]]{3}-[[:digit:]]{4}'
    || '|[[:digit:]]{3}\.[[:digit:]]{4}');
```

This expression is a bit difficult to read, because the narrow page width used in this book forces us to show it as the concatenation of two strings. The || operator is the SQL string-concatenation operator. The single | that you see beginning the second string is the regular expression alternation operator. The first half of the regular expression looks for phone numbers delimited by dashes; the second half looks for phone numbers delimited by periods.

Whenever you use alternation, it's a good idea to enclose your two alternatives within parentheses. We didn't use parentheses in our previous example, so alternative #1 consists of everything to the left of the vertical bar, and alternative #2 consists of everything to the right. Parentheses constrain alternation to just the subexpression within the parentheses, enabling you to write more concise expressions:

```
SELECT park_name
FROM park
WHERE REGEXP_LIKE(description,
    '[[:digit:]]{3}(-|\.)[[:digit:]]{4}');
```

This time the entire expression isn't repeated. The alternation is limited to specifying the alternate delimiters: (-|\.).

When an alternation involves only single characters, you really don't need to specify an alternation at all. A choice of one out of several single characters is better expressed as a bracket expression. The following example uses [-.] to allow for either a dash or a period in phone numbers:

```
SELECT park_name
FROM park
WHERE REGEXP_LIKE(description,
    '[[:digit:]]{3}[-.][[:digit:]]{4}');
```

Earlier you saw a period used to match any character, and a dash used to define a range of characters in a bracket expression. However, when used as the first character in a bracket expression, the dash represents itself. Similarly, the period always represents itself in a bracket expression. See "[ ] (Square Brackets)" in the "Regular Expression Quick Reference" section for more details on special rules in bracket expressions.

The following example makes good use of alternation to extract U.S. and Canadian phone numbers, including area codes, from park descriptions. We use alternation to deal with the two area code formats:

```
SELECT park_name, REGEXP_SUBSTR(description,
   '([[:digit:]]{3}[-.]|\([[:digit:]]{3}\) )'
   ||'[[:digit:]]{3}[-.][[:digit:]]{4}')
   park_phone
FROM park;
```

In this example, we used alternation to deal with the fact that some area codes are enclosed within parentheses. We used a bracket expression to accommodate the varying use of periods and dashes as delimiters. Parentheses enclose the area code portion of the expression, limiting the scope of the alternation to just that part of the phone number.

Greediness

Regular expressions are *greedy*. Greedy in the context of regular expressions means that a quantifier will match as much of the source string as possible.

For example, while writing this book, one of us wrote the following regular expression in an attempt to extract the first word from the source text by looking for a sequence of characters *followed by a space*. Sounds like a reasonable approach, right? Wrong!

```
SELECT REGEXP_SUBSTR(
   'In the beginning','.+[[:space:]]')
```

```
FROM dual;
```

In the

What's happened here? The first sequence of characters followed by a space is `'In '`, so why was `'In the '` returned? The answer boils down to what regular expression users refer to as *greediness*. The regular expression engine will indeed find that `'In '` matches the specified pattern, but that's not enough! The engine wants more. It's greedy. It looks to see whether it can match an even longer run of characters, and in this case it can. It can match up characters through `'In the '`, and so it does.

NOTE

The last word, `'beginning'`, is not followed by a space, and so the regular expression cannot match it.

What if you do just want that first word? One solution is to use a negated bracket expression to specify that you want to find a pattern consisting of non-spaces:

```
SELECT REGEXP_SUBSTR(
   'In the beginning','[^[:space:]]*')
FROM dual;
```

In

This time, the engine will find `'In'` and stop at the space that follows, because that space is not part of the set denoted by the bracket expression. A possibly beneficial side effect of this approach is that the result does not include a trailing space, though it would include trailing punctuation if any punctuation immediately followed the first word in the sentence.

Backreferences

Oracle supports the notion of *backreferences* in regular expressions. A backreference is a numbered reference in the form \1, \2, and so forth, to the text matching a previous subexpression.

The following query contains an example of a regular expression with a backreference, in this case \2:

```
SELECT park_name, REGEXP_SUBSTR(description,
        '(^|[[:space:][:punct:]]+)([[:alpha:]]+)'
        || '[[:space:][:punct:]]+\2'
        || '($|[[:space:][:punct:]]+)') doubled_word
FROM park
WHERE REGEXP_LIKE(description,
        '(^|[[:space:][:punct:]]+)([[:alpha:]]+)'
        || '[[:space:][:punct:]]+\2'
        || '($|[[:space:][:punct:]]+)');
```

The same regular expression appears twice in this query, and is one solution to the classic problem of finding doubled words such as 'the the' in a block of text. To help you understand this expression, we'll walk you through it one piece at a time:

(^|[[:space:][:punct:]]+)

> The first word in a sequence of doubled words must be preceded by whitespace or punctuation, be the first word following a newline line ([:space:] includes newline), or be the first word in the string. This subexpression is \1, but we do not reference it from later in the expression.

([[:alpha:]]+)

> A word is defined as a sequence of one or more alphabetic characters. This subexpression is \2.

[[:space:][:punct:]]+

> The two words in a sequence of doubled words must be separated by one or more space and punctuation characters.

\2

> The second word must be the same as the first. The subexpression defining the first word is the first subexpression, so we refer back to the value of that subexpression using \2.

```
($|[[:space:][:punct:]]+)
```
> The second word must also be followed by space and/or
> punctuation characters, be the last word in a line, or be
> the last word in the string.

Our use of \2 in this expression is key to our goal of finding
doubled words. Consider the following sentence fragment:

```
Fort Wilkins is is a ...
```

When the regular expression engine evaluates our expression in the context of this sentence, it follows these steps:

1. The engine begins by finding the beginning of the line as
   a match for the first subexpression.

2. Next, the engine tries 'Fort' as the match to the second
   subexpression. Thus \2 refers to 'Fort', and the engine
   looks for 'Fort Fort'. Instead, the engine finds 'Fort
   Wilkins'.

3. The engine moves on to try 'Wilkins' as the match for
   the second subexpression. \2 now refers to 'Wilkins' and
   the engine looks for 'Wilkins Wilkins'. Instead, the
   engine finds 'Wilkins is'.

4. The regular expression engine tries 'is' as the match for
   the second expression. \2 then refers to 'is', so the
   engine looks for 'is is' and is successful at finding a
   match.

Our example query uses two functions that you'll read more
about in the upcoming section on "Oracle's Regular Expression Support." First, REGEXP_LIKE is used to identify rows
that have doubled words in their description. Next,
REGEXP_SUBSTR extracts those doubled words for you to
review. Both functions leverage the same regular expression.

NOTE

REGEXP_LIKE is optimized to do as little as possible to
prove that an expression exists within a string.

You can reference the first nine subexpressions in a regular expression using \1, \2, etc., through \9. Subexpressions from the tenth onwards cannot be referenced at all.

Fuzziness

Pattern matching is not an exact science. Regular expressions let you search and manipulate text based on patterns. People can get very creative when it comes to variations on a pattern or making new patterns, and sometimes people don't seem to follow any pattern at all.

Think of writing a regular expression as a learning process, a chance to get to know your data better. Begin by taking your best shot at writing an expression to match the text you are after. Test that expression. Review the results. Do you find false positives? Then refine your expression to eliminate those false positives, and iterate through the testing process again. You may never be able to truly eliminate all false positives; you may have to settle for tolerating some small percentage of them.

Don't forget to review your data for false negatives, which are items containing text that you want, but which your regular expression as currently developed will exclude. Remember the periods in the phone numbers discussed in previous sections. Our first attempt at a regular expression to identify phone numbers excluded all those with periods.

Finally, don't be intimidated by the inherent *fuzziness*, as we call it, in regular expressions, nor be put off by it. Just understand it. Regular expressions are incredibly useful. They have their place and, like any other feature, they also have their own strengths and weaknesses.

Oracle's Regular Expression Support

Oracle's regular expression support manifests itself in the form of three SQL functions and one predicate that you can use to search and manipulate text in any of Oracle's supported text datatypes: VARCHAR2, CHAR, NVARCHAR2, NCHAR, CLOB, and NCLOB.

NOTE

Regular expression support does not extend to LONG, because LONG is supported only for backward compatibility with existing code.

Regular Expression Functions

Following are the four functions you'll use to work with regular expressions in Oracle:

REGEXP_LIKE
> Determines whether a specific column, variable, or text literal contains text matching a regular expression.

REGEXP_INSTR
> Locates, by character position, an occurrence of text matching a regular expression.

REGEXP_REPLACE
> Replaces text matching a regular expression with new text that you specify. Your replacement text can include backreferences to values in the regular expression.

REGEXP_SUBSTR
> Extracts text matching a regular expression from a character column, variable, or text literal.

Of these, you've already seen REGEXP_LIKE in quite a few examples. REGEXP_LIKE is documented in the "Conditions" chapter of the *Oracle Database 10g SQL Reference* because in SQL it can only be used as a predicate in the WHERE and HAVING clauses of a query or DML statement. In PL/SQL, however, you can use REGEXP_LIKE as you would any other Boolean function:

```
DECLARE
    x Boolean;
BEGIN
    x := REGEXP_LIKE(
        'Does this string mention Oracle?',
        'Oracle');
END;
/
```

The remaining three functions work identically in SQL and PL/SQL. All four functions are fully described in the "Oracle Regular Expression Functions" section near the end of this book.

Regular Expression Locale Support

Oracle is notable for its Globalization Support in that it supports an exceedingly wide variety of character sets, languages, territories, and linguistic sorts. Regular expressions are no exception. The combination of character set, language, and territory is known as a *locale*. Oracle's regular expression engine respects locale, and is configurable via NLS (National Language Support) parameter settings.

Following are some notable examples of the way in which regular expression locale support affects you:

- The regular expression engine is character-based. The period (.) will always match a single character or, more strictly speaking, a single codepoint, regardless of how many bytes are used to represent that character in the underlying character set.

- Character classes are sensitive to the underlying character set. For example, if you're using one of the Unicode character sets, the class [:digit:] will include not only 0,

---

1, 2, through 9, but also the Arabic-Indic •, ١, ٢ through ٩, the Bengali ০, ১, ২ through ৯, and so forth.

- NLS_SORT can affect how comparisons are performed. If NLS_SORT considers two characters to be equivalent, then so does the regular expression engine. For example, using the default sort of BINARY, the expression 'resume' will not match the text 'Résumé'. Change NLS_SORT to GENERIC_BASELETTER, and the expression does match, because that sort treats 'e' and 'é' as the same letter and also ignores case.

- Bracket expressions such as [A-z] are affected by the underlying character set and the sort order. For example:

  - [a-z] includes A when using the case-insensitive sort GERMAN_CI, but not when using GERMAN.

  - Given an ASCII-based character set and the BINARY sort order, [A-z] encompasses all letters, upper- and lowercase. Given an EBCDIC character set and the BINARY sort order, [A-z] fails to be a valid expression, even failing to compile, because in EBCDIC the binary representation of the letter A comes after that of the letter z.

- If a regular expression is in one character set, and the text to be searched is in another, the regular expression will be converted to the character set of the text to be searched.

- Your NLS_SORT setting affects whether case-sensitive matching is done by default. A sort such as SPANISH yields case-sensitive sorting. You can add the suffix _CI, as in SPANISH_CI, to linguistic sorts to get a case-insensitive sort. Use the suffix _AI for an accent-insensitive sort.

- NLS_SORT also affects which accented and unaccented characters are considered to be of the same class. For example, the expression 'na[[=i=]]ve' will match both 'naive' and 'naïve' when NLS_SORT is set to BINARY (the default sort for the AMERICAN language), but not when NLS_SORT is set to GREEK.

- NLS_SORT affects which collation elements are considered valid. For example, [.ch.] is recognized by Spanish sorting rules (when NLS_SORT equals XSPANISH), but not by American sorting rules.

Regular Expression Matching Options

Each of Oracle's regular expression functions takes an optional *match_parameter*, which is a character string that you can fill with one-character flags. This string gives you control over the following aspects of regular expression behavior:

Whether matching is case-sensitive
    NLS_SORT controls whether matching is case-sensitive by default, which it usually will be. You can override the default on a per-call basis.

Whether the period (.) matches newline characters
    By default, periods do not match newline characters (occurrences of CHR(10) on Unix systems) in the source text. You can specify that periods match newlines.

The definition of "line"
    By default, the source string that you are searching is considered one long line, and the caret (^) and dollar sign ($) match only the beginning and ending of the entire string.

    You can specify that the source value is to be treated as many lines delimited by newline characters. If you do so, then the ^ and $ match the beginning and end of each line respectively.

The following example demonstrates the use of the *match_parameter* by performing a case-insensitive search for doubled words. The *match_parameter* value in this case is 'i'. The two 1 parameters preceding 'i' in REGEXP_SUBSTR supply the default values for starting position and occurrence. Those parameters need to be specified in order to reach the *match_parameter*.

```
SELECT park_name, REGEXP_SUBSTR(
        description,
        '(^|[[:space:][:punct:]]+)([[:alpha:]]+)'
        || '([[:space:][:punct:]])+\2'
        || '([[:space:][:punct:]]+|$)',
        1,1,'i') duplicates
FROM park
WHERE REGEXP_LIKE(description,
        '(^|[[:space:][:punct:]]+)([[:alpha:]]+)'
        || '([[:space:][:punct:]])+\2'
        || '([[:space:][:punct:]]+|$)', 'i');
```

To specify multiple parameters, simply list them in one string. For example, to request case-insensitive matching with periods matching newline characters, specify 'in' or 'ni' as your *match_parameter*.

If you specify contradictory parameters, Oracle uses the last value in the string. For example, 'ic' is contradictory because 'i' asks for case-insensitivity, while 'c' asks for the opposite. Oracle resolves this by taking the last value in the string, in this case the 'c'.

If you specify parameters that are undefined, Oracle will return an ORA-01760: illegal argument for function error.

Standards Compliance

Oracle's regular expression engine is of the traditional non-deterministic finite automata (traditional NFA) variety, the same type used in Perl, the .NET environment, and Java. With one exception, Oracle's engine implements the syntax and behavior for extended regular expressions (EREs) as described in the POSIX standard. In addition, Oracle adds support for backreferences.

NOTE

The regular expression syntax and behavior documented in the *Open Group Base Specifications Issue 6, IEEE Standard 1003.1, 2003 Edition* is the same as that for POSIX. You can view the Open Group specifications at *http://www.opengroup.org/onlinepubs/007904975/basedefs/ xbd_chap09.html*

The one exception that stands between Oracle and full POSIX compliance is that Oracle does not attempt to determine the longest possible match for a pattern containing variations, as the standard requires. The following example demonstrates this very well:

```
SELECT REGEXP_SUBSTR('bbb','b|bb') FROM dual;

b

SELECT REGEXP_SUBSTR('bbb','bb|b') FROM dual;

bb
```

These two statements differ only by the order in which the alternatives are specified in the regular expression: b|bb versus bb|b. The longest possible match in either case is 'bb', and that's the match POSIX requires for both cases. However, Oracle's regular expression engine takes the first match it finds, which can be either 'b' or 'bb', depending on the order in which the alternatives are specified.

NOTE

Do not confuse finding the longest possible match out of several alternations with greediness.

Like many regular expression engines, Oracle ignores the "longest possible match" rule, because the overhead of computing all possible permutations and then determining which is the longest can be excessive.

Differences Between Perl and Oracle

Perl has done a lot to popularize the use of regular expressions, and many regular expression engines (e.g., Java and PHP) follow Perl's implementation closely. Many readers may have learned regular expressions using Perl or a Perl-like engine, so this brief section highlights the key differences between Perl's and Oracle's support for regular expressions.

> **NOTE**
>
> This section is based a comparison of Perl Version 5.8 with Oracle Database 10g.

String literal issues

Regular expressions are often written as string literals. When you move string literals from one language to another, you may encounter issues with the way that each language handles such literals.

For example, Perl enables you to to use \x followed by two hexadecimal digits to embed arbitrary byte codes within a string. Perl also supports character sequences such as \n for the newline (linefeed on Unix) character. Thus, in Perl, you can write the following regular expression to search for either a linefeed or a space:

```
/[\n|\x20]/
```

The issue is that this isn't a regular expression per se—it's a Perl string. The backslash sequences \n and \x20 have no meaning to Perl's regular expression engine, which, in fact, never sees them. Those sequences are interpreted by Perl itself. By the time the string gets to Perl's regular expression engine, \n and \x20 have been replaced by the appropriate byte codes.

Another issue you may encounter is Perl's use of the dollar sign ($) to dereference a variable within a string. In Perl, the expression /a$b/ searches for the letter 'a' followed by the contents of the Perl variable named b. Perl's regular expression never sees the '$b', because Perl substitutes the value of the variable before it passes the string to the engine.

Neither SQL nor PL/SQL support the use of \ and $ in the way that Perl does. Because Perl and Oracle differ in their handling of string literals, you may not be able to take a regular expression developed for Perl and simply drop it into Oracle. Before attempting to move an expression in the form of a string literal from Perl to Oracle, make sure that the "expression" doesn't contain any characters that Perl itself interprets.

NULL versus empty strings

Unlike Perl and many database products, Oracle treats an empty string as a NULL value. Thus, the following query, which attempts to match an empty string, brings back no data:

```
SELECT * FROM park
WHERE REGEXP_LIKE(description,'');
```

In Oracle, the regular expression engine does not see an empty string; rather, it sees a NULL, or the complete absence of an expression with which to do any matching.

Perl-specific syntax

Oracle's regular expression syntax is POSIX-compliant. Perl's engine supports a number of operators, character classes, and so forth that are not defined as part of the POSIX standard. These are described in Table 2. Where possible, we also specify a POSIX equivalent that's usable in Oracle.

NOTE

The POSIX equivalents shown in Table 2 should work for the default locale (American_America.US7ASCII, with a BINARY sort). However, we have not yet been able to run exhaustive tests.

Table 2. Perl's nonstandard regular expression operators

Perl operator	Description / Oracle equivalent
[[:ascii:]]	Matches any ASCII character. In Oracle, possibly use: '[' || CHR(00) || '-' || CHR(127) || ']'.
[[:word:]]	A word character, defined as any alphanumeric character, including underscore: [[:alnum:]_]
\C	Embeds arbitrary bytes in a regular expression. In Oracle, use the CHR function, but be aware that Oracle requires an expression to be composed of valid *characters* as defined by the underlying character set.
\d	Digits: [[:digit:]]
\D	Non-digits: [^[:digit:]]
\pP	Named properties, no POSIX equivalent
\PP	Negated named properties, no POSIX equivalent
\s	Whitespace: [[:space:]], except that [[:space:]] includes vertical tab (\x0B), and \s does not.
\S	Non-whitespace: [^[:space:]]
\w	Alphanumeric characters: [[:alnum:]_]
\W	Non-alphanumeric characters: [^[:alnum:]_]
\X	Followed by a code point value, \X embeds a Unicode combining character sequence into a regular expression. In Oracle, use the COMPOSE function to generate Unicode combining characters from code points.
\b \B \A \Z \z \G	Perl supports a number of zero-width assertions. None are recognized by POSIX.

Syntax Perl does not support

Perl does not support the POSIX-standard [= =] notation for defining an equivalence class. In addition, Perl does not support the use of [. .] to specify a collation element.

Negating character classes

Both Perl and Oracle support the POSIX-compliant caret (^) as the first character within a bracket expression to mean all characters except those listed within the expression. For example, you can write: [^A-Z] to match on any character but the uppercase letters.

Perl also supports the use of a caret in conjunction with a character class name. For example, Perl allows you to write [[:^digit:]] to match on any character except for one in the [:digit:] class. You can get the same effect in Oracle using the form: [^[:digit:]].

Lazy quantifiers (non-greediness)

As we described in "Greediness" in the "Tutorial" section, quantifiers in a regular expression will match as many characters as possible. For example, given a source string of '123456', the expression [0-9]+ will match the entire string of six digits.

Perl supports the addition of a question mark (?) to the end of a quantifier to make it non-greedy, or *lazy*, in which case the quantifier matches the minimum number of characters possible. For example, the expression [0-9]+? matches only the first digit of the string '123456'.

The complete list of lazy quantifiers supported by Perl is:

*?, +?, ??, and {}?

POSIX, and by extension Oracle, does not support these quantifiers.

Experimental features

Perl supports a mechanism for adding experimental regular expression features. Such features always take the form (?...), in which the ellipses represent the feature-specific syntax. Comments within expressions are one of the so-called experimental features, and you can embed a comment in a Perl regular expression as follows:

```
(?#area code)([[:digit:]]{3}[-\.]|\([[:digit:]]{3}\))
(?#local number)[[:digit:]]{3}[-\.][[:digit:]]{4}
```

Oracle does not support Perl's experimental feature syntax.

Backreferences

In a replacement string such as one you might use with REGEXP_REPLACE, Perl supports the use of a dollar sign ($) to indicate a backreference. For example, you can use $1 to refer to the first subexpression. Oracle supports only the backslash syntax \1, \2, and so forth.

Backslash differences

POSIX and Perl differ somewhat in how they handle backslash (\) characters:

\ *in a bracket-list*
> In Perl, a \ in a bracket-list is treated as a metacharacter. In Oracle, a \ in a bracket-list represents itself.

\ *as the last character of an expression*
> Use \ as the last character of a regular expression in Perl, and you get an error. Do the same thing in Oracle, and the trailing \ is silently ignored.

Regular Expression Quick Reference

This section provides a quick-reference summary of the behavior of all the regular expression metacharacters supported by Oracle.

NOTE

Most metacharacters are treated as regular characters when used within square brackets ([ ]). See the "[ ] (Square Brackets)" section for more details on this issue.

\ (Backslash)

Use the backslash (\) to treat as normal a character that would otherwise have a special meaning. For example, to extract a dollar amount from a sentence, you might escape the period (.) and the dollar sign ($) as follows:

```
SELECT REGEXP_SUBSTR(
    'This book costs $9.95 in the U.S.',
    '\$[[:digit:]]+\.[[:digit:]]+')
FROM dual;

$9.95
```

The \$ in this expression requires that the matching text begin with a dollar sign. The \. requires a period between the two digit groups.

To specify a backslash in an expression, escape it with another backslash. The following query retrieves all text up to and including the last backslash:

```
SELECT REGEXP_SUBSTR(
    'I want this \ but not this',
    '.*\\')
FROM dual;

I want this \
```

If the character following a backslash in an expression is not a metacharacter, then the backslash is ignored:

```
SELECT REGEXP_SUBSTR('\test','\test')
FROM dual;

test
```

The \ has no special meaning within square brackets ([ ]). When used within square brackets, \ represents itself.

\1 through \9 (Backslash)

References the value matched by a preceding subexpression

Use \1, \2, \3, etc. through \9 to create backreferences to values matched by preceding subexpressions. You can backreference up to nine subexpressions, the first nine, in any expression. Subexpressions are numbered in the order in which their opening parentheses are encountered when scanning from left to right.

For example, to flip a name from *last, first* format to *first last*:

```
SELECT REGEXP_REPLACE(
    'Sears, Andrew',
    '(.+), (.+)','\2 \1')
FROM dual;
```

```
Andrew Sears
```

For more examples, see "Backreferences" in the "Tutorial" section and the section on REGEXP_REPLACE under "Oracle Regular Expression Functions."

. (Period)

Matches any character

The period matches any character in the underlying character set of the string to be searched, except that by default it does not match the newline character.

The following example uses a regular expression consisting of eight periods to extract the first sequence of eight contiguous characters from a string:

```
SELECT REGEXP_SUBSTR('Do not' || CHR(10)
                   || 'Brighten the corner!'
                        ,'........')
FROM dual;
```

```
Brighten
```

These results do not include the first characters in the string, because the seventh character is a newline (CHR(10)), and that newline breaks the pattern. The first eight contiguous characters, exclusive of newlines, form the word 'Brighten'.

You can specify 'n' in the optional *match_parameter* to cause the period to match the newline:

```
SELECT REGEXP_SUBSTR('Do not' || CHR(10)
                || 'Brighten the corner!'
                  ,'.........',1,1,'n')
FROM dual;

Do not
B
```

Periods do not match NULLs, and they lose their special meaning when used within square brackets ([ ]).

---

^ (Caret)   Matches the beginning-of-line

Use the caret (^) to anchor an expression to the beginning of the source text, or to the beginning of a line within the source text.

By default, Oracle treats the entire source value as one line, so ^ matches only the very beginning of the source value:

```
SELECT REGEXP_SUBSTR(
    'one two three','^one ')
FROM dual;

one
```

If the text you're looking for isn't at the beginning of the source string, it won't be matched. The following query returns NULL:

```
SELECT REGEXP_SUBSTR(
    'two one three','^one ')
FROM dual;
```

The caret is valid anywhere within an expression. For example, the following expression matches either 'One' or 'one',

---

but in either case the word matched must come at the beginning of the string:

```
SELECT REGEXP_SUBSTR(
    'one two three','^One|^one')
FROM dual;
```

one

You can change Oracle's default behavior to treat the source text as a *set* of "lines" delimited by newline characters. You do this using the 'm' *match_parameter*, as follows:

```
SELECT REGEXP_SUBSTR(
    'three two one'
    || CHR(10) || 'one two three',
    '^one',1,1,'m')
FROM dual;
```

one

Because 'm' is used, the ^ anchors to the beginning of any line in the text, and the pattern '^one' matches the word 'one' at the very beginning of the second line.

Be careful, though, that you don't write an impossible expression such as 'one^one', which attempts to anchor the beginning of the string, or the beginning of a line within the string, to the middle of a value matched by the expression. You can only anchor the beginning of a line/string to the beginning of a value. If you want to match a value across a newline, you can take one of at least two approaches:

- Use an expression such as 'two[[:space:]]three', which works because the definition of [:space:] includes newline.

- If you specifically must have the newline character in the value, then build an expression containing the newline character, as in: 'two' || CHR(10) || 'three'.

The ^ is not a metacharacter within square brackets ([ ]), except when it is the very first character within those brackets. In such cases, it negates the remaining characters within the brackets. See the "[ ] (Square Brackets)" section for details.

$ (Dollar Sign)   Matches the end-of-line

Use the dollar sign ($) to anchor a regular expression to the end of the source text, or to the end of a line within the source text.

For example, the $ in the following query's regular expression is the reason why 'three' is returned rather than 'one':

```
SELECT REGEXP_SUBSTR(
    'one two three','(one|two|three)$')
FROM dual;
```

```
three
```

As with the caret (^), you can use 'm' to treat the source text as a series of "lines" delimited by newline (CHR(10) on Unix systems) characters.

The $ is not a metacharacter within square brackets([ ]).

[ ] (Square Brackets)   Matches any of a set of characters

Use square brackets ([]) to create a *matching list* that will match on any one of the characters in the list.

The following example searches for a string of digits by applying the plus (+) quantifier to a matching list consisting of the set of digits 0–9:

```
SELECT REGEXP_SUBSTR(
    'Andrew is 14 years old.',
    '[0123456789]+ years old')
FROM dual;
```

```
14 years old
```

A better solution to this problem is to define a range of digits using the dash (-):

```
[0-9]+ years old
```

Even better is to specify a character class:

```
[[:digits:]]+ years old'
```

Begin a list with a caret (^) to create a *non-matching list* that specifies characters to which you do *not* want to match. The following extracts all of a sentence except the ending punctuation:

```
SELECT REGEXP_SUBSTR(
    'This is a sentence.',
    '.*[^.!:]')
FROM dual;
```

```
This is a sentence
```

Virtually all regular expression metacharacters lose their special meaning and are treated as regular characters when used within square brackets. The period in the previous SELECT statement provides an example of this, and Table 3 describes some exceptions to this general rule.

Table 3. Characters that retain special meaning within square brackets

Character	Meaning
^	An initial ^ defines a non-matching list. Otherwise, the ^ has no special meaning.
-	Specifies a range, for example 0-9. When used as the very first or very last character between brackets, or as the first character following a leading ^ within brackets, the - holds no special meaning, and matches itself.
[	Represents itself, unless used as part of a character class, equivalence class, or collation. For example, use [[ ] to match just the left, square bracket ([).
]	Represents itself when it is the first character following the opening (left) bracket ([), or the first character following a leading caret (^). For example, use [ ] [ ] to match opening and closing square brackets; use [^] [ ] to match all but those brackets.
[: :]	Encloses a character class name, for example [:digit:].
[. .]	Encloses a collation element, for example [.ch.].
[= =]	Encloses an equivalence class, for example [=e=].

[. .] (Collation Element)

Use [. and .] to enclose a collation element, usually a multicharacter collation element. Collation elements must be specified within bracket expressions.

The following example uses the collation element [.ch.] to find a word containing the Spanish letter 'ch' with a case-insensitive search. First, look at the results when we simply place the letters 'c' and 'h' in a bracket expression:

```
ALTER SESSION SET NLS_LANGUAGE=SPANISH;
SELECT REGEXP_SUBSTR(
   'El caballo, Chico come la tortilla.',
   '[[:alpha:]]*[ch][[:alpha:]]*',1,1,'i')
FROM dual;
```

```
caballo
```

These aren't the results we want! Even though 'ch' is two letters, Spanish, at least old Spanish, treats it as one. Collation elements let us deal with this situation:

```
ALTER SESSION SET NLS_SORT=XSPANISH;
SELECT REGEXP_SUBSTR(
   'El caballo, Chico come la tortilla.',
   '[[:alpha:]]*[[.ch.]][[:alpha:]]*',1,1,'i')
FROM dual;
```

```
Chico
```

By specifying the collation [.ch.] in the bracket expression, we tell the regular expression engine to look for the combination 'ch', not for a 'c' or an 'h'. We also had to change our NLS_SORT setting from SPANISH (the default for the Spanish language) to XSPANISH in order for the collation to be recognized. This is because SPANISH uses modern rules that treat 'ch' as two letters, but XSPANISH uses older rules that treat 'ch' as one letter.

Technically, any single character is a collation element. Thus,
[a] and [[.a.]] are equivalent. In practice, you only need to
use collation element syntax when a collation element consists of multiple characters that linguistically represent one
character. Table 4 provides a list of such cases recognized by
Oracle. The collation elements in the table are only valid for
the specified NLS_SORT settings.

Table 4. Collation elements

NLS_SORT	Multicharacter collation elements
XDANISH	aa AA Aa oe OE Oe
XSPANISH	ch CH Ch ll LL Ll
XHUNGARIAN	cs CS Cs gy GY Gy ly LY Ly ny NY Ny sz SZ Sz ty TY Ty zs ZS Zs
XCZECH	ch CH Ch
XCZECH_PUNCTUATION	ch CH Ch
XSLOVAK	dz DZ Dz dž DŽ Dž ch CH Ch
XCROATIAN	dž DŽ Dž lj LJ Lj nj Nj NJ

[: :] (Character Class)

Use [: and :] to enclose a character class name, for example: [:alpha:]. Character classes must be specified within bracket expressions, as in [[:alpha:]].

The following example uses the character class [:digit:] to match the digits in a ZIP code:

```
SELECT REGEXP_SUBSTR(
    'Munising MI 49862',
    '[[:digit:]]{5}') zip_code
FROM dual;
```

```
49862
```

In this example, we could just as well have used the pattern [0-9]{5}. However, in multilingual environments digits are not always the characters 0–9. The character class [:digit:] matches the English 0–9, the Arabic-Indic •–٩, the Tibetan ०–९, and so forth.

Table 5 describes the character class names recognized by Oracle. All names are case-sensitive.

Table 5. Supported character classes

Class	Description
[:alnum:]	Alphanumeric characters (same as [:alpha:] + [:digit:])
[:alpha:]	Alphabetic characters only
[:blank:]	Blank space characters, such as space and tab
[:cntrl:]	Nonprinting or control characters
[:digit:]	Numeric digits
[:graph:]	Graphical characters (same as [:punct:] + [:upper:] + [:lower:] + [:digit:])
[:lower:]	Lowercase letters
[:print:]	Printable characters
[:punct:]	Punctuation characters
[:space:]	Whitespace characters such as space, form-feed, newline, carriage return, horizontal tab, and vertical tab

Table 5. Supported character classes (continued)

Class	Description
[:upper:]	Uppercase letters
[:xdigit:]	Hexadecimal characters

[= =] (Equivalence Class) Specifies an equivalence class

Use [= and =] to surround a letter when you want to match all accented and unaccented versions of that letter. The resulting equivalence class reference must always be within a bracket expression. For example:

```
SELECT REGEXP_SUBSTR('eéëèÉËÈE' '[[=É=]]+')
FROM dual;
```

eéëèÉËÈE

```
SELECT REGEXP_SUBSTR('eéëèÉËÈE', '[[=e=]]+')
FROM dual;
```

eéëèÉËÈE

It doesn't matter which version of a letter you specify between the [= and =]. All equivalent accented and unaccented letters, whether upper- or lowercase, will match.

NOTE

NLS_SORT determines which characters are considered to be equivalent. Thus, equivalence can be determined appropriately for whatever language you are using.

---

* (Asterisk) Matches zero or more

The asterisk (*) is a quantifier that applies to the preceding regular expression element. It specifies that the preceding element may occur zero or more times.

The following example uses ^.*$ to return the second line of a text value.

```
SELECT REGEXP_SUBSTR('Do not' || CHR(10)
                     || 'Brighten the corner!'
                     ,'^.*$',1,2,'m')
FROM dual;

Brighten the corner!
```

The 'm' *match_parameter* is used to cause the ^ and $ characters to match the beginning and end of each line, respectively. The .* matches any and all characters between the beginning and end of the line. The first match of this expression is the string "Do not". We passed a 2 as the fourth parameter to request the second occurrence of the regular expression.

If the previous element is a bracket expression, the asterisk matches a string of zero or more characters from the set defined by that expression:

```
SELECT REGEXP_SUBSTR('123789',
                     '[[:digit:]]*')
FROM dual;

123789
```

Likewise, the preceding element might be a subexpression. In the following example, each fruit name may be followed by zero or more spaces, and we are looking for any number of such fruit names:

```
SELECT REGEXP_SUBSTR('apple apple orange wheat',
      '((apple|orange|pear)[[:space:]]*)*')
FROM dual;

apple apple orange
```

Watch out! The asterisk can surprise you. Consider the following:

```
SELECT REGEXP_SUBSTR('abc123789def',
                     '[[:digit:]]*')
FROM dual;
```

The result of executing this query will be a NULL. Why? Because [[:digit:]] is optional. When the regular expression engine looks at the first character in the string (the letter 'a') it will decide that, sure enough, it has found zero or more digits, in this case zero digits. The regular expression will be satisfied, and REGEXP_SUBSTR will return a string of zero characters, which in Oracle is the same as a NULL.

+ (Plus Sign)   Matches one or more

The plus (+) is a quantifier that matches one or more occurrences of the preceding element. The plus is similar to the asterisk (*) in that many occurrences are acceptable, but unlike the asterisk in that at least one occurrence is required.

The following is a modification of the first example from the previous section on the asterisk. This example also returns the second line of a text value, but the difference is that this time .+ is used to return the second line containing characters.

```
SELECT REGEXP_SUBSTR('Do not' || CHR(10)
                || CHR(10)
                || 'Brighten the corner!'
                ,'^.+$',1,2,'m')
FROM dual;
```

```
Brighten the corner!
```

The first line is 'Do not', and is skipped because the fourth parameter requests line two. The second line is a NULL line, which is skipped because it contains no characters. The third line is returned from the function because it's the second occurrence of the pattern: a line containing characters.

Just as the asterisk can be applied to bracket expressions and subexpressions, so can the plus. Unlike the asterisk, the plus will not match on a NULL. Following is a modification of the query in the preceding section that returned a NULL, but this time the + quantifier is used:

```
SELECT REGEXP_SUBSTR('abc123789def',
                '[[:digit:]]+')
```

```
FROM dual;
```

```
123789
```

Because + is used, the expression will not match on the NULL string preceding the letter a. Instead, the regular expression engine will continue on through the source string looking for one or more digits.

? (Question Mark)   Matches zero or one

The question mark (?) is very similar to the asterisk (*), except that it matches at most one occurrence of the preceding element. For example, the following returns only the first fruit:

```
SELECT REGEXP_SUBSTR('apple apple orange wheat',
       '((apple|orange|pear)[[:space:]]*)?')
FROM dual;
```

```
apple
```

Like the *, the ? can surprise you by matching where you don't expect. In this case, if the string doesn't begin with a fruit name, the ? will match on the empty string. See the "* (Asterisk)" section for an example of this kind of behavior.

{ } (Curly Braces)   Matches a specific number of times

Use curly braces ({}) when you want to be very specific about the number of occurrences an operator or subexpression must match in the source string. Curly braces and their contents are known as *interval expressions*. You can specify an exact number or a range, using any of the forms shown in Table 6.

Table 6. Forms of the { } interval expression

Form	Meaning
{m}	The preceding element or subexpression must occur exactly *m* times.

Table 6. Forms of the { } interval expression (continued)

Form	Meaning
{m,n}	The preceding element or subexpression must occur between m and n times, inclusive.
{m, }	The preceding element or subexpression must occur at least m times.

The following example, taken from the "Tutorial" section, uses curly braces to specify the number of digits in the different phone number groupings:

```
SELECT park_name
FROM park
WHERE REGEXP_LIKE(description,
    '[[:digit:]]{3}-[[:digit:]]{4}');
```

Using the {m,n} form, you can specify a range of occurrences you are willing to accept. The following query uses {3,5} to match from three to five digits:

```
SELECT REGEXP_SUBSTR(
        '1234567890','[[:digit:]]{3,5}')
FROM dual;
```

```
12345
```

Using {m,}, you can leave the upper end of a range unbounded:

```
SELECT REGEXP_SUBSTR(
        '1234567890','[[:digit:]]{3,}')
FROM dual;
```

```
1234567890
```

Vertical Bar (|)   Delimits alternative possibilities

The vertical bar (|) is known as the *alternation operator*. It delimits, or separates, alternative subexpressions that are equally acceptable.

For example, the expression in the following query extracts the name of a fruit from a sentence. In this example the fruit is 'apple', but any of the three listed fruits: 'apple', 'apricot', or 'orange' is equally acceptable as a match:

```
SELECT REGEXP_SUBSTR(
    'An apple a day keeps the doctor away.',
    'apple|apricot|orange')
FROM dual;

apple
```

It's usually wise to constrain your alternations using parentheses. For example, to modify the previous example to return the entire string, you could use:

```
SELECT REGEXP_SUBSTR(
    'An apple a day keeps the doctor away.',
    'An apple a day keeps the doctor away.' ||
    '|An apricot a day keeps the doctor away.' ||
    '|An orange a day keeps the doctor away.')
FROM dual;
```

This solution works, but it's painfully repetitive and does not scale well. If there were two words that could change in each sentence, and if each word had three possibilities, you'd need to write $3 \times 3 = 9$ alternate versions of the sentence. The following approach is much better, and easier:

```
SELECT REGEXP_SUBSTR(
    'An apple a day keeps the doctor away.',
    'An (apple|apricot|orange) a day ' ||
    'keeps the doctor away.')
FROM dual;
```

By constraining the alternation to just that part of the text that can vary, we eliminated the need to repeat the text that stays the same.

NOTE

An expression such as (abc|) is valid, and will match either 'abc' or nothing at all. However, using (abc)? will look less like a mistake, and will make your intent clearer.

( ) (Parentheses)

Place parentheses (( )) around a portion of a regular expression to define a subexpression. Subexpressions are useful for the following purposes:

- To constrain an alternation to the subexpression.
- To provide for a backreference to the value matched by the subexpression.
- To allow a quantifier to be applied to the subexpression as a whole.

The regular expression in the following example uses parentheses twice. The innermost set constrains the alternation to the three fruit names. The outermost set defines a subexpression in the form of *fruit name + space*, which we require to appear from 1 to 3 times in the text.

```
SELECT REGEXP_SUBSTR(
    'orange apple pear lemon lime',
    'orange ((apple|pear|lemon)[[:space:]]){1,3}')
FROM dual;
```

```
orange apple pear lemon
```

See the "Tutorial" section, especially under "Alternation" and "Backreferences," for more examples showing the use of parentheses in regular expressions.

Oracle Regular Expression Functions

Oracle's regular expression support, which we introduced earlier in the book, manifests itself in the form of four functions, which are described in this section. Each function is usable from both SQL and PL/SQL.

All the examples in this section search text literals. We do this to make it obvious how each function works, by showing you both input and output for each example. Typically, you do not use regular expressions to search string literals, but rather to search character columns in the database, or character variables in PL/SQL.

For the same reason, the regular expressions in this section are simple to the extreme. We don't want you puzzling over our expressions when what you really want is to understand the functions.

REGEXP_INSTR   Locates text matching a pattern

REGEXP_INSTR returns the beginning or ending character position of a regular expression within a string. You specify which position you want. The function returns zero if no match is found.

Syntax

```
REGEXP_INSTR(source_string, pattern
             [, position [, occurrence
             [, return_option
             [, match_parameter]]]])
```

All parameters after the first two are optional. However, to specify any one optional parameter, you must specify all preceding parameters. Thus, if you want to specify match_parameter, you must specify all parameters.

Parameters

source_string
    The string you want to search.

pattern
    A regular expression describing the text pattern you are searching for. This expression may not exceed 512 bytes in length.

position
    The character position at which to begin the search. This defaults to 1, and must be positive.

---

occurrence

> The occurrence of *pattern* you are interested in finding. This defaults to 1. Specify 2 if you want to find the second occurrence of the pattern, 3 for the third occurrence, and so forth.

return_option

> Specify 0 (the default) to return the pattern's beginning character position. Specify 1 to return the ending character position.

match_parameter

> A set of options in the form of a character string that change the default manner in which regular expression pattern matching is performed. You may specify any, all, or none of the following options, in any order:

> `'i'`

> > Specifies case-insensitive matching.

> `'c'`

> > Specifies case-sensitive matching.

NOTE

The NLS_SORT parameter setting determines whether case-sensitive or -insensitive matching is done by default.

> `'n'`

> > Allows the period (.) to match the newline character. Normally, that is not the case.

> `'m'`

> > Causes the caret (^) and dollar sign ($) to match the beginning and ending, respectively, of lines within the source string. Normally, the caret (^) and dollar sign ($) match only the very beginning and very ending of the source string, regardless of any newline characters within the string.

Examples

Following is an example of a simple case, in which the string 'Mackinac', commonly misspelled 'Mackinaw', is located within a larger string:

```
SELECT REGEXP_INSTR(
    'Fort Mackinac was built in 1870',
    'Mackina.')
FROM dual;
```

6

If you're interested in the ending character position, actually one past the ending position, you can specify a value of 1 for *return_option*, which forces you to also specify values for *position* and *occurrence*:

```
SELECT REGEXP_INSTR(
    'Fort Mackinac was built in 1870',
    'Mackina.',1,1,1)
FROM dual;
```

14

The *occurrence* parameter enables you to locate an occurrence of a pattern other than the first:

```
SELECT REGEXP_INSTR(
    'Fort Mackinac is near Mackinaw City',
    'Mackina.',1,2)
FROM dual;
```

23

The following example uses *position* to skip the first 14 characters of the search string, beginning the search at character position 15:

```
SELECT REGEXP_INSTR(
    'Fort Mackinac is near Mackinaw City',
    'Mackina.',15)
FROM dual;
```

23

For an example involving *match_parameter*, see "Regular Expression Matching Options" in the "Tutorial" section.

REGEXP_LIKE Determines whether a given pattern exists

REGEXP_LIKE is a Boolean function, or predicate, which returns true if a string contains text matching a specified regular expression. Otherwise REGEXP_LIKE returns false.

Syntax

```
REGEXP_LIKE (source_string, pattern
            [, match_parameter])
```

Parameters

source_string

    The string you want to search.

pattern

    A regular expression describing the text pattern you are searching for. This expression may not exceed 512 bytes in length.

match_parameter

    A set of options in the form of a character string that change the default manner in which regular expression pattern matching is performed. You may specify any, all, or none of the following options, in any order:

    'i'

        Specifies case-insensitive matching.

    'c'

        Specifies case-sensitive matching.

NOTE

The NLS_SORT parameter setting determines whether case-sensitive or -insensitive matching is done by default.

'n'

Allows the period (.) to match the newline character. Normally, that is not the case.

'm'

Causes the caret (^) and dollar sign ($) to match the beginning and ending, respectively, of lines within the source string. Normally, the caret (^) and dollar sign ($) match only the very beginning and very ending of the source string, regardless of any newline characters within the string.

Examples

In a SQL statement, REGEXP_LIKE may be used only as a predicate in the WHERE and HAVING clauses. This is because SQL does not recognize the Boolean data type. For example:

```
SELECT 'Phone number present'
FROM DUAL
WHERE REGEXP_LIKE(
        'Tahquamenon Falls: (906) 492-3415',
        '[0-9]{3}[-.][0-9]{4}');
```

In PL/SQL, REGEXP_LIKE may be used in the same manner as any other Boolean function:

```
DECLARE
    has_phone BOOLEAN;
BEGIN
    has_phone := REGEXP_LIKE(
        'Tahquamenon Falls: (906) 492-3415',
        '[0-9]{3}[-.][0-9]{4}');
END;
/
```

REGEXP_LIKE, and even the other regular expression functions, can also be used in CHECK constraints. The following constraint ensures that phone numbers are always stored in (xxx) xxx-xxxx format:

```
ALTER TABLE park
ADD (CONSTRAINT phone_number_format
```

```
CHECK (REGEXP_LIKE(park_phone,
'^\([0-9]{3}\) [0-9]{3}-[0-9]{4}$')));
```

For an example involving *match_parameter*, see "Regular
Expression Matching Options" in the "Oracle's Regular
Expression Support" section.

REGEXP_REPLACE
Replaces text matching a pattern

REGEXP_REPLACE searches a string for substrings matching a regular expression, and replaces each substring with
text that you specify. Your replacement text may contain
backreferences to subexpressions in the regular expression.
The new string, with all replacements made, is returned as
the function's result.

REGEXP_REPLACE returns either a VARCHAR2 or a
CLOB, depending on the input type. The return value's character set will match that of the source string.

Syntax

```
REGEXP_REPLACE(source_string, pattern
              [, replace_string
              [, position [, occurrence
              [, match_parameter]]]])
```

All parameters after the first two are optional. However, to
specify any one optional parameter, you must specify all preceding parameters. Thus, if you want to specify *match_
parameter*, you must specify all parameters.

Parameters

source_string
    The string containing the substrings that you want to
    replace.

pattern
    A regular expression describing the text pattern of the
    substrings you want to replace. Maximum length is 512
    bytes.

replace_string

The replacement text. Each occurrence of *pattern* in *source_string* is replaced by *replace_string*. See "Back-references" later in this section for important information on using regular expression backreferences in the replacement text.

Maximum length is 32,767 bytes. Any replacement text value larger than 32,767 bytes will be truncated to that length.

NOTE

If you're using multibyte characters, truncation might result in less than 32,767 bytes, because Oracle will truncate to a character boundary, never leaving a partial character in a string.

Up to 500 backreferences are supported in the replacement text. To place a backslash (\) into the replacement text, you must escape it, as in \\.

position

The character position at which to begin the search-and-replace operation. This defaults to 1, and must be positive.

occurrence

The occurrence of *pattern* you are interested in replacing. This defaults to 0, causing *all* occurrences to be replaced. Specify 1 if you want to replace only the first occurrence of the pattern, 2 for only the second occurrence, and so forth.

match_parameter

A set of options in the form of a character string that change the default manner in which regular expression pattern matching is performed. You may specify any, all, or none of the following options, in any order:

'i'

> Specifies case-insensitive matching.

'c'

> Specifies case-sensitive matching.

NOTE

The NLS_SORT parameter setting determines whether case-sensitive or -insensitive matching is done by default.

'n'

> Allows the period (.) to match the newline character. Normally, that is not the case.

'm'

> Causes the caret (^) and dollar sign ($) to match the beginning and ending, respectively, of lines within the source string. Normally, the caret (^) and dollar sign ($) match only the very beginning and very ending of the source string, regardless of any newline characters within the string.

Examples

Following is an example of the simplest type of search-and-replace operation, in this case correcting any misspellings of the name Mackinaw City:

```
SELECT REGEXP_REPLACE(
    'It''s Mackinac Bridge, but Mackinac City.',
    'Mackina. City', 'Mackinaw City')
FROM dual;
```

```
It's Mackinac Bridge, but Mackinaw City.
```

By default, all occurrences of text matching the regular expression are replaced. The following example specifies 2 for the *occurrence* argument, so that only the second occurrence of the pattern 'Mackina.' is replaced:

```
SELECT REGEXP_REPLACE(
    'It''s Mackinac Bridge, but Mackinac City.',
```

```
     'Mackina.', 'Mackinaw',1,2)
FROM dual;
```

It's Mackinac Bridge, but Mackinaw City.

For an example of the *position* argument's use, see REGEXP_INSTR. For an example involving *match_parameter*, see "Regular Expression Matching Options" in the "Tutorial" section.

Backreferences

REGEXP_REPLACE allows the use of regular expression backreferences in the replacement text string. Such backreferences refer to values matching the corresponding subexpressions in the `pattern` argument.

The following example makes use of backreferences to fix doubled word problems:

```
SELECT park_name, REGEXP_REPLACE(description,
       '([[:space:][:punct:]]+)([[:alpha:]]+)'
       || '([[:space:][:punct:]]+)\2'
       || '[[:space:][:punct:]]+',
       '\1\2\3') description
FROM park
WHERE REGEXP_LIKE(description,
       '([[:space:][:punct:]]+)([[:alpha:]]+)'
       || '([[:space:][:punct:]]+)\2'
       || '[[:space:][:punct:]]+');
```

Look carefully at the subexpressions in the pattern expression, and you'll see that the subexpressions have the following meanings:

\1

The space and punctuation preceding the first occurrence of the word. This we keep.

\2

The first occurrence of the doubled word, which we also keep.

\3

The space and punctuation following the first occurrence, which we also keep.

The second occurrence of the doubled word, and whatever space and punctuation that follows it, are arbitrarily discarded.

NOTE

While the pattern shown in this section is an interesting way to rid yourself of doubled words, it may or may not yield correct sentences.

See "Backreferences" in the "Tutorial" section for a more comprehensive explanation of backreferences.

REGEXP_SUBSTR

Extracts text matching a pattern

REGEXP_SUBSTR scans a string for text matching a regular expression, and then returns that text as its result. If no text is found, NULL is returned.

Syntax

```
REGEXP_SUBSTR(source_string, pattern
              [, position [, occurrence
              [, match_parameter]]])
```

All parameters but the first two are optional. However, to specify any optional parameter, you must specify all preceding parameters. Thus, when specifying *match_parameter*, all other parameters are also required.

Parameters

source_string
The string you want to search.

pattern

> A regular expression describing the pattern of text you want to extract from the source string.

position

> The character position at which to begin searching. This defaults to 1.

occurrence

> The occurrence of *pattern* you want to extract. This defaults to 1.

match_parameter

> A set of options in the form of a character string that change the default manner in which regular expression pattern matching is performed. You may specify any, all, or none of the following options, in any order:

> `'i'`
>
>> Specifies case-insensitive matching.

> `'c'`
>
>> Specifies case-sensitive matching.

NOTE

The NLS_SORT parameter setting determines whether case-sensitive or -insensitive matching is done by default.

> `'n'`
>
>> Allows the period (.) to match the newline character. Normally, that is not the case.

> `'m'`
>
>> Causes the caret (^) and dollar sign ($) to match the beginning and ending, respectively, of lines within the source string. Normally, the caret (^) and dollar sign ($) match only the very beginning and very ending of the source string, regardless of any newline characters within the string.

Examples

The following example extracts U.S. and Canadian phone numbers from park descriptions:

```
SELECT park_name, REGEXP_SUBSTR(description,
    '(([[:digit:]]{3}[-.]|\([[:digit:]]{3}\) )'
    ||'[[:digit:]]{3}[-.][[:digit:]]{4}')
    park_phone
FROM park;

PARK_NAME                   PARK_PHONE
-------------------------   --------------
Färnebofjärden              ***NULL***
Mackinac Island State Park  517-373-1214
Fort Wilkens State Park     (800) 447-2757
...
```

This PL/SQL-based example loops through the various phone numbers in a description:

```
<<local>>
DECLARE
   description park.description%TYPE;
   phone VARCHAR2(14);
   phone_index NUMBER;
BEGIN
   SELECT description INTO local.description
   FROM park
   WHERE park_name = 'Fort Wilkins State Park';

   phone_index := 1;

   LOOP
      phone := REGEXP_SUBSTR(local.description,
         '(([[:digit:]]{3}[-.]|\([[:digit:]]{3}\) )'
         ||'[[:digit:]]{3}[-.][[:digit:]]{4}',
         1,phone_index);

      EXIT WHEN phone IS NULL;
      DBMS_OUTPUT.PUT_LINE(phone);
      phone_index := phone_index + 1;
   END LOOP;
END;
/

(800) 447-2757
```

```
906.289.4215
(906) 289-4210
```

The key to this example is that phone_index is incremented following each match, causing REGEXP_SUBSTR to iterate through the first, second, and third phone numbers. Iteration stops when a NULL return value indicates that there are no more phone numbers to display.

Oracle Regular Expression Error Messages

The following list details Oracle errors specific to regular expressions, and suggests how you might resolve them.

ORA-01760: illegal argument for function

This is not strictly a regular expression error. However, you can get this error if you pass an invalid *match_parameter* to one of the REGEXP functions. See "Regular Expression Matching Options" in the "Oracle's Regular Expression Support" section for more details.

You can also get this error by passing an invalid type for any parameter. For example, you'll get this error if you pass a number where a string is expected, or vice-versa.

If you do get this error as the result of a call to one of the REGEXP functions, check to be sure that all your argument types are valid, and that you are passing only valid matching options ('i', 'c', 'm', or 'n') in your *match_parameter* argument, which is always the last argument of a REGEXP function call.

ORA-12722: regular expression internal error

Contact Oracle Support and open a Technical Assistance Request (TAR), because you've encountered a bug.

ORA-12725: unmatched parentheses in regular expression

You have mismatched parentheses in your expression. For example, an expression like '(a' will cause this error. Carefully check each subexpression to be sure you include both opening and closing parentheses. Check to see whether you've correctly escaped parentheses that do not enclose subexpressions, and make sure you haven't inadvertently escaped a parentheses that should open or close a subexpression.

ORA-12726: unmatched bracket in regular expression

You have mismatched square brackets in your expression. Apply the advice we give for ORA-12725, but this time look at your use of square brackets. Also, while an expression such as '[a' will cause this error, an expression such as 'a]' will not, because a closing (right) bracket is treated as a regular character unless it is preceded by an opening (left) bracket.

ORA-12727: invalid back reference in regular expression

You wrote a backreference to a subexpression that does not exist, or that does not yet exist. For example, '\1' is invalid because there is no subexpression to reference. On the other hand, '\1(abc)' is invalid because the backreference precedes the subexpression to which it refers. Verify that all your backreferences are valid, and that they always refer to *preceding* subexpressions.

ORA-12728: invalid range in regular expression

You specified a range, such as '[z-a]', in which the starting character does not precede the ending character. Check each range in your expression to ensure that the beginning character precedes the ending character. Also check your NLS_SORT setting, as it is NLS_SORT that determines the ordering of characters used to define a range.

ORA-12729: invalid character class in regular expression:

You specified an invalid character class name within [: and :].
Check your regular expression to be sure you are using only
those names valid for your release of Oracle. Table 4 in the
"Regular Expression Quick Reference" section lists names valid
for the initial release of Oracle Database 10g.

ORA-12730: invalid equivalence class in regular expression

You specified a sequence of characters within [= and =] that
cannot be resolved to a single base letter. For example,
[=ab=] is not a valid two-character equivalence.

ORA-12731: invalid collation class in regular expression

You specified a collation element that does not exist in your
current sort order. For example, specifying [.ch.] when
NLS_SORT is other than XSPANISH or XCZECH will cause
this error, because other languages never treat the combination 'ch' as a single character. Check your expression to be
sure that each use of [= and =] is valid, and check your NLS_
SORT setting.

ORA-12732: invalid interval value in regular expression

Using curly braces, you specified a range of repeat counts in
which the beginning of the range is greater than the end. For
example, '{3,1}' is invalid because 3 is greater than 1.
Within curly braces, the smallest value must come first (e.g.,
'{1,3}').

CPSIA information can be obtained at www.ICGtesting.com
Printed in the USA
266031BV00004B/4/P